SHOW JUMPING

by

Jane Wallace

Illustrations by

Carole Vincer

KENILWORTH PRESS

First published in Great Britain by
The Kenilworth Press Limited,
Addington, Buckingham, MK18 2JR

© The Kenilworth Press Limited 1992

Reprinted 1993

British Library Cataloguing in Publication Data
A catalogue record for this book is available from the British Library.

ISBN 1-872082-36-X

Typeset by Alacrity Phototypesetters, Banwell Castle,
Weston-super-Mare, Avon

Printed in Great Britain by Westway Offset, Wembley

CONTENTS ■ ■ ■ ■ ■ ■ ■ ■ ■ ■ ■

Introduction

Show jumping is a test of a horse's obedience and his athletic ability. Correct jumping is only possible if the horse is well schooled on the flat. Dressage and jumping therefore go hand in hand. In order for a horse to use himself to the maximum in an agile and athletic way, he must be supple and disciplined so that he is physically and mentally able to respond to his rider's wishes.

The object of show jumping is for a horse to be able to negotiate a course of varied, non-fixed obstacles without faults. The object of training is to make this possible. The better trained the horse, the more chance he has of jumping fences without a problem. The rider must understand what is necessary on the approach to a fence so that he can help his horse without interfering.

The keynotes to all jumping are **rhythm, balance** and **impulsion.** Provided that your horse can work well on the flat, he should have no trouble in reproducing equally good work whilst jumping.

Many riders find cross-country jumping far easier than show jumping. This is because the increased speed of the cross-country gives impetus (as opposed to impulsion, which is required by the slower speed of show jumping). The impetus gives a wider range of take-off points, which allows for less accurate riding. A horse can tap a solid cross-country fence without doing damage to himself, but if he taps a show-jumping pole, he will invariably incur penalties.

To replace speed with impulsion, the horse has to be able to bring his hocks underneath him and be able to carry weight on his hindquarters. He must be able to canter in a balanced way and be able to maintain this canter on the approach to a fence. The rider must ride forwards, maintain rhythm and balance but without restricting the horse on the approach to every fence. The less the rider interferes, the better!

Tack and equipment

All tack and clothing must fit, be comfortable and safe.

It is important to use a jumping saddle which not only fits the horse well, but also gives the rider support for his position when jumping a fence. A good numnah will help to cushion the horse's back.

A running martingale is a useful item – you hope you will never need it, but it is there just in case. Provided that the running martingale is correctly fitted, the horse will be unaware of it – that is, unless he puts his head in a position which makes him out of control, then the martingale comes into action. Anyway, you should always use either a martingale, breastplate or breastgirth to hold the saddle in position – especially useful in an emergency such as if the saddle slips due to a loose girth.

The girth should be of strong material such as double webbing, leather or nylon. Lampwick girths are liable to snap and are not safe. A surcingle gives extra security and should always be used in competition.

Stirrups must be made of steel, preferably stainless, and not nickel which is a soft metal and will bend. They must be the correct size. Stirrup leathers should be made of rawhide, a leather which will stretch but not break.

Rubber-covered reins give grip when the neck of the horse becomes wet, but do not use re-rubbered reins for jumping because they are weak. Ensure that bridle billets are securely fastened and check regularly for signs of wear.

Always wear a crash-cap when jumping, however small the fences. Jodhpur boots or riding boots are also essential. Never wear trainers or shoes without a heel – being dragged is every rider's nightmare.

RUNNING MARTINGALE

CRASH-CAP WITH SILK

WHITE SHIRT AND TIE

TWEED JACKET

NUMNAH

TENDON BOOTS

OVER-REACH BOOTS

SURCINGLE

YORKSHIRE BOOTS

This horse's legs are well protected with front and hind boots. The rider is wearing competition dress, which is both smart and practical.

The horse's jumping technique

CORRECT TECHNIQUE – GOOD ACTION IN FRONT AND BEHIND

INCORRECT TECHNIQUE – FRONT AND HIND LEGS DANGLING

A horse must gather his energy in order to spring into the air. On the approach to a fence, the horse must be balanced, in a rhythmical pace and have enough impulsion to jump; the bigger the fence, the more energy and spring required.

The final stride before take-off should be a little shorter than the preceding ones, because this is when the horse gathers himself to take off. If the last couple of strides are longer, the horse is likely to fall onto his forehand and so arrive at the point of take-off in an unbalanced state. For a successful jump the horse's forehand must be light and his weight should be on his hocks.

When one talks of a horse's technique over a fence, it means how he folds his legs in the air and his style of jumping. Good foreleg technique is particularly important in an event

horse, who is unlikely to fall if he hits a fence behind, but will probably do so if he raps a solid fence hard with his forelegs. A show jumper needs good technique all round to be successful. A horse with good foreleg technique is quick to lift his knees and tightly fold his forelegs. Some horses even need a shield to protect the stomach against injury from shoe studs, so tightly do they fold their legs. Poor technique in front means that the horse leaves either one or both knees down when he jumps.

In good hind leg technique the horse lifts his stifles and stretches out his hind leg so that he can clear both upright and spread fences. A horse who does not lift his hindquarters and so trails his hind legs is likely to knock down fences, similarly a horse who tucks his hind feet underneath him.

A horse is described as having scope when he gives the impression that he can jump a high and wide fence with ease. A horse who struggles to jump a wide fence and tucks his hind legs under him lacks scope.

The rider's position

Left: Typical faults in rider position. Both are unbalanced and incorrect and as such will hinder the horse in his efforts to jump the fence.

Right: Here the rider is exhibiting a good, secure position over the fence, giving the horse the freedom he needs to jump cleanly.

The position of the rider is important, not only over the fence, but also on the approach and the landing.

On the approach, the rider must keep his body still to help the horse remain in balance all the way to the fence. If the rider leans forward in the last few strides before a fence, he is likely to transfer extra weight onto the horse's forehand, so making it more difficult for the horse to lift his shoulders up into the air. The rider must allow the horse to keep coming forward to the fence and not restrict him with his hand. Rhythm, balance and impulsion are the vital ingredients for jumping.

Over the top of the fence, the rider must swing forward straight and not to one side. He must keep the weight in his stirrup, with the heel down. If the rider's heel comes up, he loses the security of his seat and then relies on the horse for balance. If the rider uses the horse's neck and shoulders for support, he makes the jump more difficult for the horse.

The rider should feel that although he and the horse are 'as one', the horse is free to jump in balance underneath him, and he is not relying on the horse for his own balance. An independent seat means that the rider is able to give the horse as much head and neck freedom as he requires.

The rider should look between the horse's ears towards the next fence, and keep his head up. The rider's seat should be just above the saddle once the horse has taken off. If the weight is still in the saddle, the horse will be forced to hollow his back.

On landing, the rider should keep his heels down to maintain balance and security and allow the horse to use his head and neck for balance as he lands.

Schooling at home on the flat

Schooling on the flat for jumping should follow the same pattern as for dressage itself (see also *Flatwork Exercises* in this series). The ultimate aim is a well-trained horse who is supple, obedient and athletic. The better schooled the horse is on the flat, the easier he will be to ride and consequently the better he will be able to perform. Any stiffness on the flat will be more apparent when the horse jumps and, in fact, any imperfections in the flatwork will be magnified once the horse starts to jump.

In order to achieve a supple horse, he should be worked on circles, changes of bend with serpentines, transitions and increases and decreases of pace. These exercises all help to improve the carrying and propelling power of the hocks and the suppleness of the horse through his back and ribs. It is important to work a horse equally on both reins and to aim for a well-balanced horse who can carry himself. Any resistance against the rider's hand should be avoided and corrected.

A good exercise which helps to perfect turns into fences, is turning up the centre line. Aim to be absolutely straight and precise. Discipline yourself and your horse to turn onto an exact line without overshooting or wandering. This reproduces a turn into a fence, when it is equally important to turn as precisely as in a dressage arena.

The horse must be able to lengthen and shorten his stride without losing rhythm and balance and, of course, without fighting the rider's hand. It is only when the work on the flat is correct and established that the horse will be able to produce fluent jumping technique.

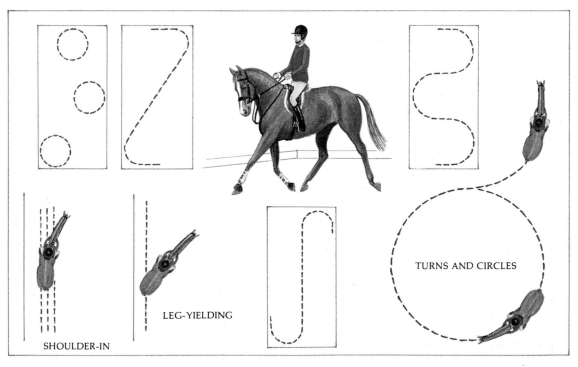

SHOULDER-IN

LEG-YIELDING

TURNS AND CIRCLES

Schooling at home over fences

As with most skills, jumping requires practice for both horse and rider. If there is a problem at home, it will become worse in a competition, not better. Do not avoid things which you or your horse find difficult – work on them and practise them until they are perfected.

Trotting poles provide a good, athletic exercise for the horse. They improve suppleness and balance and exercise all the joints of the horse by making him lift his legs higher.

Gridwork is of enormous benefit. A simple cross pole to a parallel (shown right) is the most basic but also one of the most useful exercises. A trot pole places the horse correctly for take-off for the cross pole, and a pole between the two fences ensures that the horse takes a stride (the distance is short) and that the stride is round and the horse does not hollow his back. The short distance encourages the horse to jump the parallel correctly and helps improve his technique.

Jumping grids is much easier than jumping fences from canter, but make sure that you practise both. Your horse should not be over-jumped, though – twice a week for about half an hour is not excessive. During these training sessions, you should incorporate some gridwork and also jumping fences from canter. Vary the type of fence you jump and build doubles, combinations and related distances (see later). Practise jumping fences on the angle, and also turn short into schooling fences so that the horse is not suddenly taken by surprise at a show when you jump against the clock.

For safety reasons, always have someone with you when you jump.

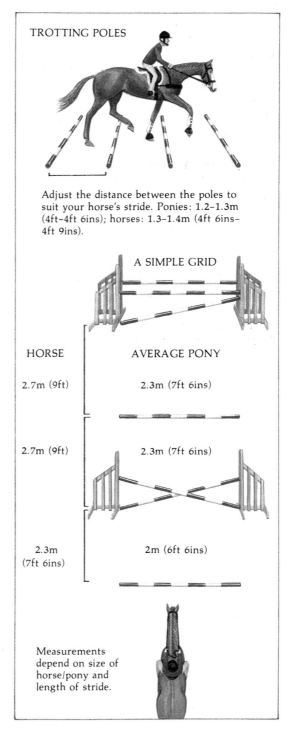

TROTTING POLES

Adjust the distance between the poles to suit your horse's stride. Ponies: 1.2–1.3m (4ft–4ft 6ins); horses: 1.3–1.4m (4ft 6ins–4ft 9ins).

A SIMPLE GRID

HORSE	AVERAGE PONY
2.7m (9ft)	2.3m (7ft 6ins)
2.7m (9ft)	2.3m (7ft 6ins)
2.3m (7ft 6ins)	2m (6ft 6ins)

Measurements depend on size of horse/pony and length of stride.

Walking the course

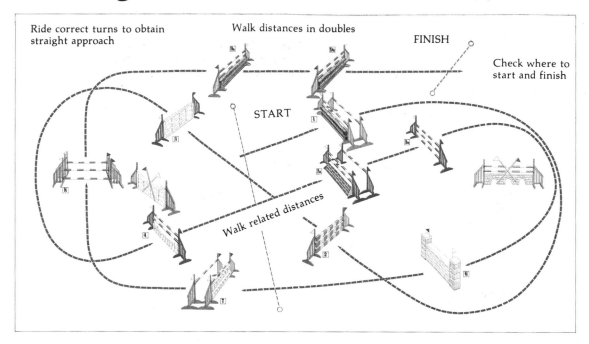

Ride correct turns to obtain straight approach

Walk distances in doubles

FINISH

Check where to start and finish

START

Walk related distances

The rider should take full advantage of this chance to familiarise himself with the layout of the fences and the fences themselves. It is a time to concentrate and will be of little benefit if it is spent chatting to friends on the way. It is only too easy to miss out a fence or take the wrong route, so it is worth spending time memorising the track and the fences. Many a class has been lost by elimination for an error of course.

Apart from the overall course route, the turns into the fences should be studied. Decide how far you need to swing out to arrive on a good line into the fences. Remember that time faults are costly and if you choose a wide route on every corner, you risk exceeding the time.

Walk the line that you will ride and imagine, as you walk round, that you are in fact riding your horse. Walk related distances and distances between double or treble elements and note any peculiarities in the going or terrain.

After you have walked the course once, stand and study the fences and go through them again in your mind. In an important competition, it is a good idea to walk the course twice, if not three times, so that you thoroughly know the course. When you return to your horsebox, sit down quietly and visualise your ride round the course, jumping every fence.

Make sure that you know exactly where the start and finish are and find out what the start sound is – it might be a horn, whistle, bell or buzzer. Golden rule: 'Wait for the bell'.

Clear rounds are often thrown away by careless course walking, so concentrate when walking!

The approach

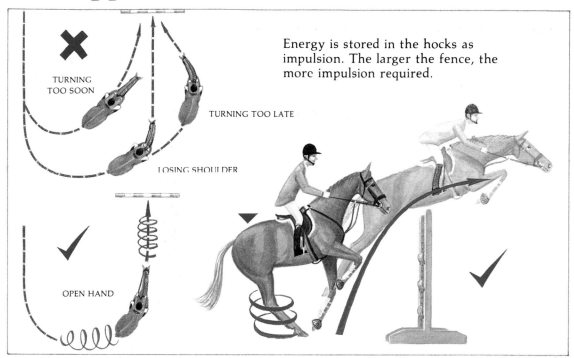

TURNING TOO SOON

TURNING TOO LATE

LOSING SHOULDER

OPEN HAND

Energy is stored in the hocks as impulsion. The larger the fence, the more impulsion required.

The approach to a fence includes not only the line taken to it, but also the way in which the horse arrives at the fence for take-off.

The line to a fence must be straight. It should be at right angles to the fence and directed to the centre of the fence itself. (In special cases this may differ – see p.17, alternating parallels.) When jumping against the clock, the horse is asked to jump fences on the angle, but this is only when the horse is more advanced in his work and sufficiently experienced to be able to do it. In the first round, which is not against the clock, the horse must be given every opportunity to weigh up his fences and must be correctly presented at all of them. As when driving a car, or riding a bicycle, you do not look at the steering wheel or handle bars when deciding where to turn, instead you

look ahead. The same applies in riding a horse. Turn your head and allow your eyes to lead you to where you want to go. The moment you look down you lose forward movement and wander off the true line.

In order to jump any fence, the horse must have energy (impulsion) stored ready for take-off. The bigger the fence, the more impulsion required. On the approach to each fence the rider must ensure that the horse is cantering with a forward, rhythmical, balanced canter which is full of impulsion. As soon as the horse has landed from a fence, the rider should try to pick up this canter again as soon as possible.

Remember that the landing of one fence becomes the approach to the next. Study the top show jumpers and note how they keep perfect rhythm and balance throughout their rounds.

How to ride an ascending spread

In an ascending spread the front pole is slightly lower than the back pole. This fence is not as difficult for the horse as a true (square) parallel because he does not have to be quite so quick and neat in his technique. He can make a slightly flat jump and still clear the fence.

A spread fence may be built of just poles, or it may incorporate planks in front with a pole as the back rail. (A fence should never have a plank as a back rail.) It may be built with a pole behind a wall and the fence may have fillers to make it appear more solid.

Being more imposing than an upright, the horse finds it easier to judge his take-off. The horse will respect a well-built fence and so jump it better than an insignificant obstacle.

Riders know that impulsion is necessary to jump a spread and so they tend to ride with more determination, which in turn makes the horse jump with more effort. Although you should create more impulsion for a spread fence, do not be tempted to make the horse increase his pace just before the fence. Keep your legs on strongly, but maintain the rhythm all the way to take-off. If you allow the horse to lengthen his stride or quicken, there is a danger that he will fall onto his forehand and so lose balance. Once the weight has fallen onto the horse's shoulders, he will have little chance of clearing the fence.

Use the corners to create impulsion and then a series of half-halts to help drive the horse's hocks under him on the approach.

Think 'rhythm and balance' and allow the fence to come to you.

How to ride a parallel

A parallel or square oxer has a front and back pole at the same height. This places a demand on the horse's technique as well as his jumping ability and power. He must be quick and neat with his forelegs to clear the front rail and be able to 'open out' behind to clear the back rail as well. If he is slow to fold his forelegs, he will hit the front pole. If he trails his hind legs, he will hit the front pole; if he cramps behind, he will hit the back pole.

A parallel is the greatest test of a horse's scope. A horse with limited ability will struggle to jump a large square oxer.

In order for a horse to jump both the height (to clear the front pole) and the width (to clear the back pole) he must be well balanced and have plenty of impulsion. This is where schooling plays a major part. A badly trained horse will invariably have problems with fences which require accuracy.

On the approach, the rider must aim to have the horse in a good rhythm, with his hocks well under him and in perfect balance. Any resistance in the horse's mouth will indicate that he is unbalanced and not on his hocks.

Unless the horse is working correctly on the approach, he will be unable to alter his stride pattern to meet the fence correctly for take-off. Provided that the horse has rhythm, balance and impulsion, he will be able to shorten or lengthen his stride and still be able to clear the fence. The range of take-off points is not so great with parallels as with ascending spreads so this also increases the difficulty of jumping them.

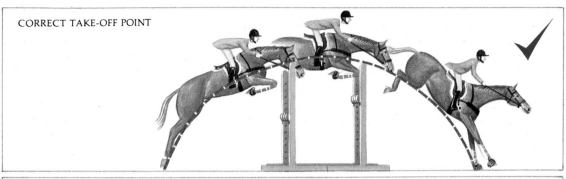

CORRECT TAKE-OFF POINT

INCORRECT TAKE-OFF POINT

CORRECT TAKE-OFF POINT

INCORRECT TAKE-OFF POINT

How to ride a triple bar

A triple bar is a staircase fence where three sets of wings support poles at progressively higher settings. A small filler can replace the front pole and this gives the fence a more solid appearance than only poles.

A triple bar does not demand good technique from the horse's front legs, but he must be able to 'open out' behind to clear the back pole.

To jump the width, a slight increase in pace may be necessary but the horse must not fall onto his forehand in doing so. If the horse lacks impulsion, he will struggle to make the width, so the rider must make sure that he has plenty of 'petrol in the tank' on the approach.

When riding towards a triple bar, the best pole on which to focus is the middle one. If you ride to that pole,

there is less chance of you asking the horse to take off too far away. If this did happen, the horse would then have a huge width to jump, and there is a danger that he could land in the middle of the fence. This might make him worry about triple bars in the future.

The rider should aim to create as much impulsion as possible and maintain it all the way to the fence so that the horse can shorten his stride if necessary.

When a triple bar has a filler as the front pole, the rider must be aware of the fact that the horse will 'back off' more than if it were poles alone. The more imposing appearance means that even more impulsion is necessary on the approach to counteract any hesitation on the horse's behalf. However, a triple bar is an inviting fence and normally causes no problems.

How to ride an upright

An upright fence can be constructed from a variety of materials. It may be made simply of poles or planks; it could be a gate or a wall, or just poles with a filler below.

A horse judges his take-off point from the ground line. In an upright fence, the ground line is on the same plane as the fence itself. This makes it difficult for the horse to judge the take-off, and as a consequence upright fences are more likely to be knocked down than, for example, ascending spreads.

On the approach, the rider should aim for rhythm, balance and impulsion. However, he must remember that, as with any difficult fence, greater emphasis is laid on correctness and any lack of balance or rhythm, or a lack of impulsion, will cause problems.

Always remember that a horse does not like to hit fences, and on the whole will only do so if poorly presented. It is important that you, as a rider, do not tense up on the approach in the effort to make your horse clear the fence. Do not be tempted to 'lift' the horse on take-off. This will only force him to hollow and a knock-down will surely result. Similarly, forcing the horse to lose his rhythm by over-collecting the energy on the approach is also a recipe for failure.

The rider must sit up on the approach and take care that he does not incline his body forward in the last few strides. In other words, he should sit still and maintain rhythm and balance all the way to the fence. This gives the horse the greatest chance of clearing an upright.

CORRECT TAKE-OFF POINT ✓

INCORRECT TAKE-OFF POINT ✗

CORRECT TAKE-OFF POINT ✓

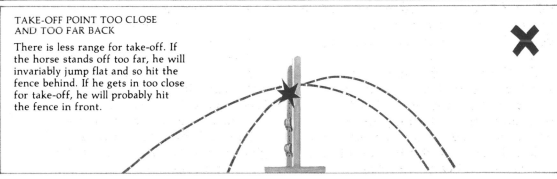

TAKE-OFF POINT TOO CLOSE
AND TOO FAR BACK ✗

There is less range for take-off. If the horse stands off too far, he will invariably jump flat and so hit the fence behind. If he gets in too close for take-off, he will probably hit the fence in front.

How to jump a stile

A 'true' stile is made of white poles
with a mock foot support at the base.
Its role in a course is as a narrow fence
and as such may also be constructed as
a wall, a gate or even a set of plank-
type rails.

It is a difficult fence to jump clear.
The narrowness of the fence distracts
the horse on the approach and he may
well be looking for a way round it. Also
the fence itself is not imposing, which
makes judgment for take-off difficult
for the horse. If the horse hesitates
momentarily, wondering if he really
has to jump through such a narrow
gap, he will lose forward movement. By
doing so he loses his rhythm, balance
and impulsion. However brief this
moment might be, it will be sufficient
to cause the horse to be unable to jump
the stile without hitting it.

A stile is therefore a true test of a
horse's training and obedience. An
untrained horse or 'green' youngster
will find this type of fence difficult due
to the fact that he is not yet completely
between the rider's hand and leg, i.e.
he can wander off a straight line at will
and is not yet able to maintain rhythm
and balance sufficiently well.

One of the most crucial factors when
attempting to jump a narrow fence is
that the line of approach must be one
hundred per cent straight and aiming
towards the middle of the fence. There
is no room for error or inaccurate
riding here. Once on the correct line,
the rider should concentrate on keeping
the essential rhythm and balance all the
way to take-off. On no account should
the rider 'lift' the horse to take off, but
he should keep the contact, albeit soft,
until take-off. 'Dropping' the horse is
a real invitation for him to run out.

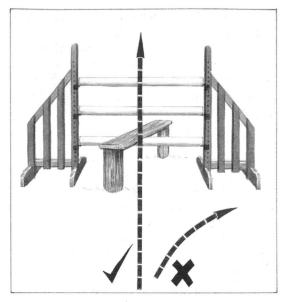

Correct approach to a stile. The line of
approach must be 100% straight. There is
no room for error.

Helsinki gate. Treat this fence as if it is a
stile.

How to jump an alternating parallel

An alternating parallel is a spread fence whose poles are crossed. It is an inviting fence to jump provided that the line of approach is correct. The fence is normally constructed with a filler in front, which adds to the solid appearance.

At this fence you can deviate from the rule of always jumping every fence in the middle. You should choose a line which converts the fence into an ascending spread as opposed to a square oxer. For example, if the front pole is higher on the left as you approach it, the back pole will be higher on the right. If you jump the fence in the middle, the horse is in danger of catching the angled front pole with his left foreleg. Horses are more likely to hit fences in front than behind, so by taking a line slightly to the right of centre, although the back rail is gradually getting higher, the horse should clear it. He will make a bigger jump to clear the back pole with his forelegs, and provided that he does not hollow in the air, the parabola should allow him to clear the back pole behind.

If the front pole of the fence is higher on the right, the line of approach should be slightly to left of centre. The line of approach must, of course, be at right angles to the fence, i.e. straight.

A problem can arise if your horse jumps to one side as he takes off. This is a bad habit, but nevertheless a common one. Horses jump to one side or the other to avoid using themselves correctly. It is a difficult problem to cure. If you know that your horse does not always jump straight, bear this in mind when deciding on your line to fences like this. Practise at home to find the best solution.

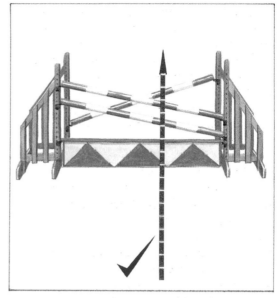

Aim for a line slightly to the right of centre when the pole is higher on the left in front. This makes the fence an ascending spread.

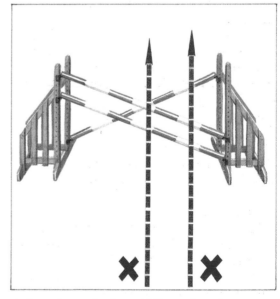

A line through the middle makes the fence into a true parallel and more difficult to jump. Too far to the right means the back pole is too high.

Doubles and combinations

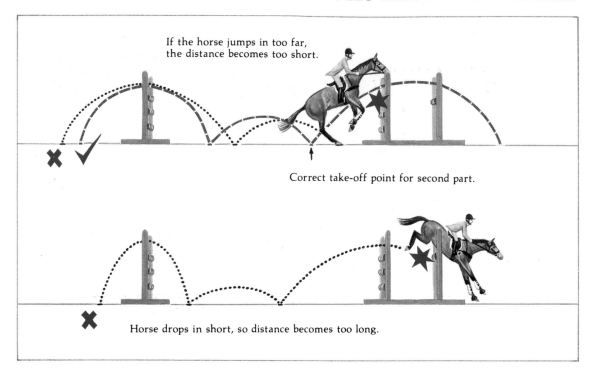

If the horse jumps in too far, the distance becomes too short.

Correct take-off point for second part.

Horse drops in short, so distance becomes too long.

Basic Coursebuilding, also in this series, explains in detail the distances for one- and two-stride doubles for horses and ponies. As a rider, you should know how to stride out a distance between elements of doubles and combinations. It is important that you are consistent with your own stride length when pacing out distances to measure the number of strides your horse will take. This takes practice and experience. Measure out the true distance of a one-stride double applicable to your horse/pony and practise striding the distance until you know what length of stride you should take.

As a rough guide, for a horse a one-stride double will 'walk' eight of your strides. A two-stride double will 'walk' eleven strides. In order to decide whether the distance is short or long, you must know the 'feel' of eight or

eleven strides.

When walking a distance, always keep your eyes down. Do not look at the fence ahead because your eyes will encourage your legs to cheat so that you meet the distance exactly.

When one or more fences are linked together, they require athleticism and power from the horse. He must be presented correctly at the first element so that he is able to jump the subsequent ones.

It is important that the horse jumps well over the first part of a double or combination because this determines how he will jump the other elements. The more impulsion the horse has on the approach, the more chance he has of meeting the first part on a good stride. This means that the rider must not over-ride so that he interferes with the rhythm or balance.

Related distances

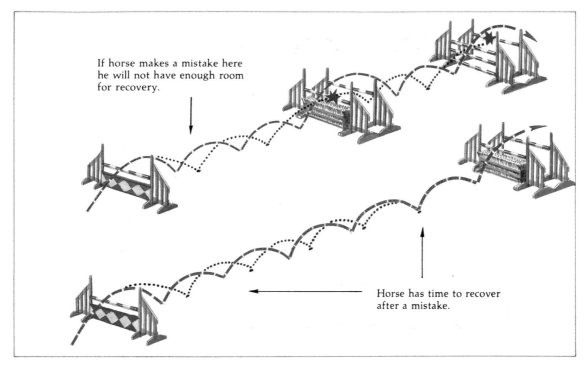

If horse makes a mistake here he will not have enough room for recovery.

Horse has time to recover after a mistake.

Basic Coursebuilding will also allow you to find details of all the measurements for related distances. Fences are said to be at a related distance when two or more are built more than two non-jumping strides apart. When fences are closer together than this, they are called doubles or combinations.

On average, a horse's stride is 12 feet (3.6m) long and a pony's stride 9 feet (2.7m). But when pacing out related distances remember the factors which lengthen or shorten a horse's stride (see p.24).

It is useful to watch several horses jumping a related distance to see how it is riding. Be careful that you are not misled by horses different from your own. A related distance will not ride well if the horse makes a mistake at the first part. He will either land too

far in or too short which makes the following distance either too short or too long.

Related distances are a test of the horse's training and his ability to adapt to a set stride pattern if it does not match his own. This is why we spend so long on flat work, teaching the horse to shorten and lengthen his stride without resistance or loss of rhythm and balance.

The rider's job is to maintain rhythm, balance and impulsion throughout the line of fences. As soon as he has landed, the horse must pick up his rhythm and balance again as soon as possible and the rider should use the half-halt to recover impulsion.

Related distances should be part of your training at home so that the horse is happy to adjust as necessary.

Collecting ring procedure – warming up ■

EXAMPLES OF PRACTICE FENCES PERMITTED UNDER BSJA RULES.

EXAMPLES OF PRACTICE FENCES NOT PERMITTED UNDER BSJA RULES.

False groundline   False groundline   Pole not in cup

The object of working the horse before a show-jumping round is to prepare him physically and mentally for what he is about to be asked to do. A young horse will probably be quite fresh at his first few shows, so it may take some time to settle him before he is ready to concentrate. The pattern of work should be a series of suppling exercises which stretch the horse's back muscles and bring his hocks under him. Unless the horse is supple and loose on the flat, he will be unable to use himself correctly when jumping. It is important to work the horse until he is relaxed but without wearing him out.

A small cross pole in trot is an ideal first fence. At an affiliated show it is not permitted, under BSJA rules, to use a placing pole for warming up.

Once the horse has popped over a cross pole a couple of times, he can be asked to canter over a small upright. At every fence, the rider must be aiming for rhythm and balance, increasing the impulsion as the size of the fence increases.

After a few upright fences, the horse can then progress to an oxer. A cross pole in front keeps the horse straight and is a good idea for the initial couple of jumps. The fence can then be changed to an ascending spread and then a square oxer. Make sure you ask your horse to jump as big as he is to jump in the ring – height as well as width.

To finish, jump an upright fence to make the horse concentrate and make a round jump.

If you have to wait a long time before it is your turn, have another jump just before you go into the ring.

Knock-downs

Horses will hit fences for many reasons. The rider must decide why his horse is unable to clear fences because until he understands what the problem is, he will be unable to rectify it.

A horse will hit a fence because it is almost impossible for him to jump it correctly, due to rider error or the horse's weakness or lack of training: rarely because the horse is clumsy. Problems on the approach to a fence invariably lead to a knock-down. This may be because the horse is not going forward, rushing, crooked, fighting his rider, stiff in his back, lacking impulsion or spooking at the fence.

Poor technique (see p.6) will increase the chances of a horse knocking down fences because the margin for error becomes far less. Unfortunately it can be said that ninety per cent of knock-downs are rider error. Lack of training may cause a long-term fault, whereas interference on the approach or a crooked line is an immediate fault. Outside influences, such as the going being slippery or a distraction, may have a bearing on whether a horse jumps his fences clear. This is particularly the case with a young, inexperienced horse.

Any physical discomfort will restrict a horse's jumping ability. This may stem from the horse's back, feet or mouth, for example, and make him reluctant to jump athletically. If a horse hollows over a fence, he is likely to hit it.

Never hit your horse if he knocks a fence. Work out why he has hit it – if you feel he was lazy, then it was **your fault** to allow him to approach a fence without enough impulsion!

Forelegs trailing. Poor technique coupled with a lack of training increases the chances of fences being hit.

This horse is jumping hollow and stiffness in his back means his hind legs are trailing.

Refusals

The reasons for a horse refusing are as numerous as those for knocking down fences. They can range from disobedience and lack of training, to genuine fear. Correct flatwork is important and unless a horse can canter to a fence in rhythm and balance with his hocks engaged, he has little chance of jumping well.

A very green, young horse may stop at a fence through suspicion. He may spook and eventually refuse, not understanding that he has to jump over something which appears rather frightening. Once the young horse has accepted that it is safe for him to jump over one brightly coloured fence, he should happily jump similar hazards.

Poor presentation, such as the horse being brought in too fast, without enough impulsion, on the angle, or being interfered with by the rider 'hooking' on the approach, all come under the heading of rider error.

Slippery conditions underfoot may cause a horse to lose his confidence. He may slip as he goes to take off – although provided that a horse is balanced, he should not slip. Studs should always be used when jumping outdoors to give extra grip.

Overfacing a horse will invite refusals, and a horse who has been overfaced in the past may become ungenerous and display moments of disobedience.

A tired horse has every reason to stop; similarly a horse in discomfort of any kind.

A rider who is half-hearted in his approach will soon give the message to his horse that he lacks determination, and any horse will soon take advantage of this. The rider must stay in balance with the horse between hand and leg until take-off. Dropping the contact at the last minute leads to refusals.

Introducing a young horse to a show

Before a young horse is taken to a show, he must be obedient to the rider's aids. Although the horse may be green and his training at a basic level, the rider must have the rudiments of control. If the horse is totally untrained, the rider will not be able to prevent him from being disobedient. Once the young horse knows how to be naughty and that he can get away with it, he will try again in the future. A horse must know that he must do as he is told.

Make sure that your young horse is not under-worked or too fresh before going to his first show. Work him quite hard at home the preceding few days so that he is not over-exuberant when he meets the excitement of other horses, flags, loud-speakers and all the other stimuli.

Work him in away from the other horses and try to warn other competitors that he is a youngster. Only when he has settled should you go into the jumping practice area. Give him plenty of time to jump the practice fence, but do not exhaust him by jumping too much. Young horses' energy levels are quite low.

For the horse's first few shows the fences should be very small so there is no chance of him frightening himself.

When it is your turn to enter, trot your horse round the fences in the ring without obviously showing them to him. You might like to trot him between the elements of the double or past a particularly spooky filler. Then trot or canter quietly round the course, bearing in mind that you are teaching your horse and he must learn to stay in rhythm as best he can.

Let your horse stand by the ringside and watch other competitors jumping.

Final thoughts

- The better the training on the flat, the better the show jumping will be.
- Rhythm, balance and impulsion are the key words, both on the flat and when jumping.
- Do not hurry your young horse. Do not gallop him against the clock or you will spoil his jump.
- Adverse ground conditions put extra premium on correct training and good riding.
- Imposing, solidly built fences jump better than flimsy, airy ones.
- Horses always jump better towards home – be prepared to ride more strongly away from home.
- Avoid giving your horse a fright either at home or in the ring – think before you jump.
- Remember that a horse's stride will **shorten** if he is going away from home, if he is going uphill slightly, if the area is confined (such as indoors), or if the going is deep or sticky. It will **lengthen** if he is going towards home, if he is going downhill slightly (he will prop if the slope is steep), if the jumping area is unrestricted or if the going is perfect.
- Always use studs when jumping outdoors to give extra grip.
- Always be sensibly and practically dressed when jumping. **Always** wear a crash cap. **Never** ride in trainers.
- Be patient – if your horse makes a mistake, ask yourself the reason why before blaming him. It was probably your fault!